The Coup De Grâce

AF441069

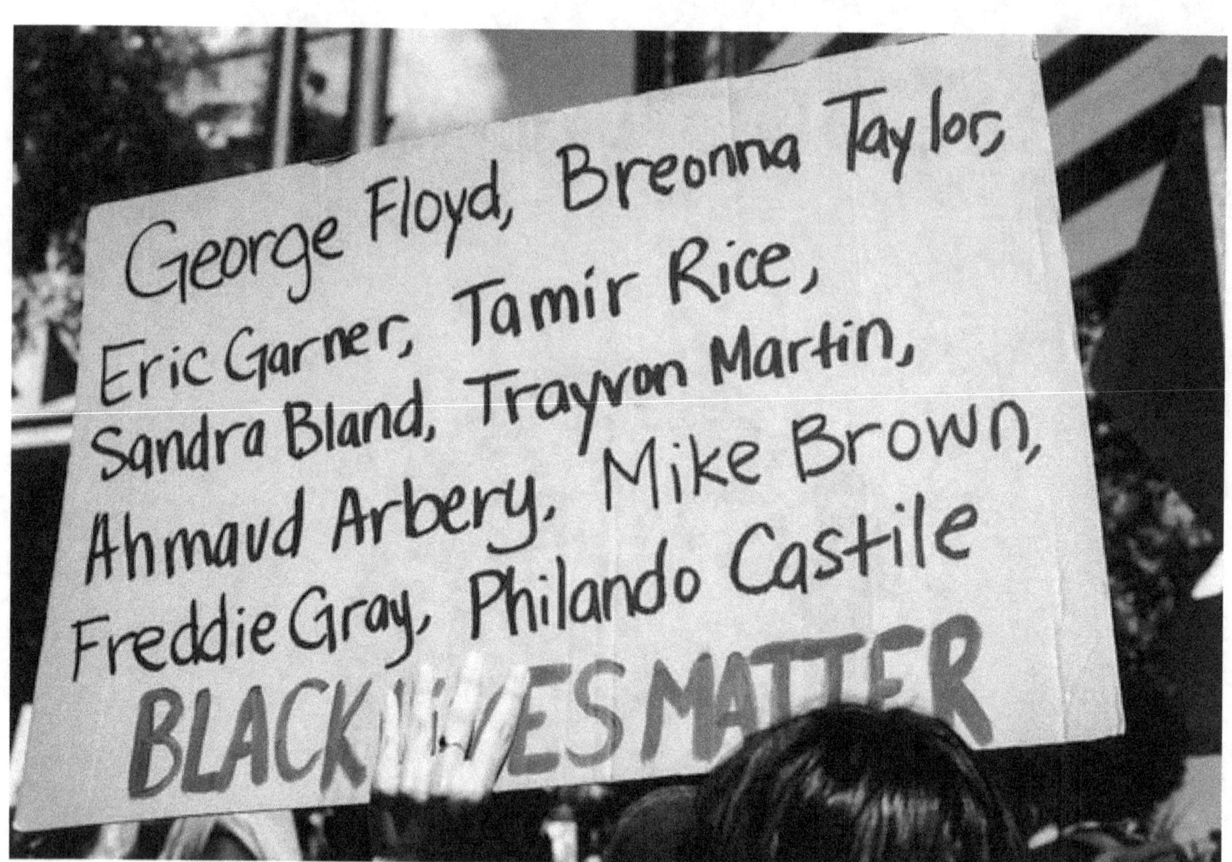

Photography Frankie Cordoba

Photography Kalea Morgan

Photography C. Shorter

Photography Maria Oswalt

Photog
raphy Maria Oswalt

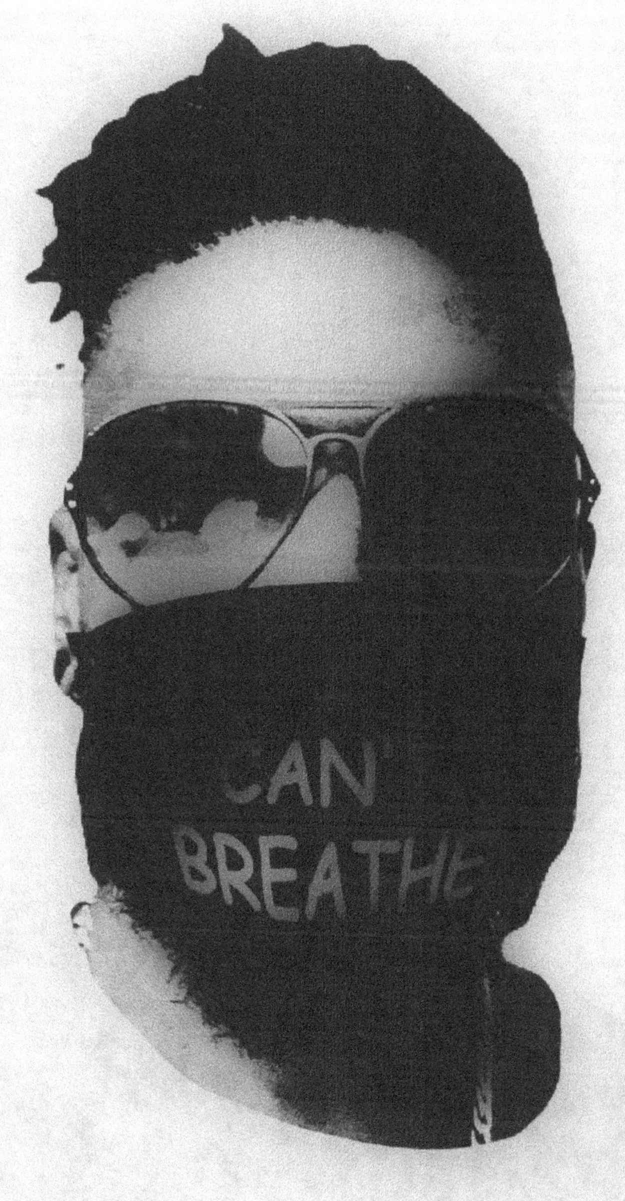

CAN'
BREATHE

Photography by James Eades

Jenius Copyright © 2020 All rights reserved ISBN: 9798686375987

This book is dedicated to the good in humanity. We shall rise together and overcome all racial injustice as one! The time has come for all who stand for good to rise!

WOKE

Okay everybody settle down ….

Everybody settle down!!!

Wake up! Your sleep, its 'bout to get real deep!

It is time for you,

And u and u and u and u and u and u,

 2 see what is going on….

Over two hundred thousand died from a pandemic,

Black men shot by police,

Systemic, Racism, Hate-ism, State-ism,

Listen up yall this that Wake-ism!

Shout out to my white folk with us in the struggle,

Bring in the clowns but make sure they can juggle,

 All my red, brown, yellow and my purple folk,

If they pick at your culture and they always make jokes and stuff, 2gether we stand divide we fall,

They tried to tell me to shut up and dribble!!

But I do not play basketball.

Make America America again??

Before they took, the land and killed all the Indians,

Before the locked asylum seekers in cages,

America should build a wall against racists,

Bigotry, Hatred! Police Brutality, Kaepernick's a Patriot!!

Wake up your sleep, its 'bout to get real deep It's time for you, and u and u and u and u and u and u, 2 see what's going on….

Wake up your sleep, its 'bout to get real deep It's time for you, and u and u and u and u and u and u, 2 see what's going on….

Photography by Kalea Morgan

"JUST US"

No justice, no peace,

Fire all the bad police,

We want justice but not "just us",

Tired of sitting in the back of the bus....

If my skin being black is a weapon to u,

All the hatred deep inside makes you do what u do,

Like showing no more remorse when you shoot seven times,

Jacob had no and his children inside,

Got your knee on my neck when I say I cannot breathe,

Every day I wonder if you will do that to me,

Or maybe you will break down my door down with a no knock,

Pull the trigger while you are calling me a ...,

No justice no peace fire all the bad police,

We want justice but not "just us", Tired of sitting in the back of the bus...

Or maybe you will just gun me down,

Saying you feel threatened and you stood your ground,

All because I had on a sweater with a hoodie,

I told 'em that you lied, and they said why would he?

 Unarmed on the ground with my hands up,

Still you pull the trigger wow man what the is up,

Playing with a toy gun, pull up on a child now his life is done.

No justice no peace,

Fire all the bad police,

We want justice but not "just us", Tired of sitting in the back of the bus....

Photography by Noah Eleazar

Photo by John Rodriguez

I CAN'T BREATHE

I can't breathe,

Take your hands up off me,

Why can't you see that.??

I can't breathe,

Why are you doing this to me?

Trans-Atlantic middle passage,

Sold like cattle across this atlas, Beat and murdered lynched and herded, Not the story that you headed.

Raped our women, Stole our children,

Sold to cotton's higher bidder, Built this country with our hands,

Refuse to even call us man! Now we stand at the day of reckoning,

Made your bed now you sleep in it! Civil Rights?

We marched in peace! Martin, Malcolm now deceased.

I can't breathe,

Take your hands up off me,

Why can't you see that.??

I can't breathe,

Why are you doing this to me? Civil Rights?

Marched in peace! Martin, Malcolm now deceased

Tried to kneel! Tried to heal! All still do not see how we feel. Pull us over every day, Treat us all any kind a way!

London Bridge is falling Everybody gather round!

Cause we will not take it anymore,

It is time for us to settle the score, By any means necessary!

And not just in February, In God we trust front seat of the bus!

Reparations for all of us! Dirty cops must be fired!

Locked in jail! And never hired… Mr. Officer! Mr. Officer!

 What seems to be the problem? Why you pull me over?

I just came from work and I am kind of tired!

Heading to my second job and I am kind of tired!

So, what you stop me for? This is profiling Just tell the truth! Black while driving!

 Why you got your gun out?

Who you plan on shooting? First you said I am speeding!

Now you say I am looting! Hmmm,

My hands are on the steering wheel,

 Your yelling at me cussing at me,

 Tempting me to keep it real!

Now its 20 cops and someone said I got a gun!

I got 20 minutes supposed to be at work by one… (Gun shots fired….)

I can't breathe,

Take your hands up off me,

Why can't you see that.??

 I can't breathe,

Why are you doing this to me?

I can't breathe,

Take your hands up off me,

Why can't you see that.??

 I can't breathe,

Why are you doing this to me?

Photography Logan Weaver

Noah Eleazar

BLACK LIVES MATTER

Black! Black! Black Lives Matters,

Black Lives Matter!! Black,

Black! Black Lives Matters, Black Lives Matter!

 This that new black national anthem,

Turn this up cause this is jamming

Ain't against the stars and stripes Its bout the black and whites,

Trying to get this thing right Let me shed the light,

First thing first let us start with slavery,

400 years of my people's bravery,

Stolen from Africa kidnapped in chains,

Displaced on these so-called fruitful plains,

Forced to pick cotton we were never compensated,

Poverty and slavery are family related, Spit on lynched, tortured and hated,

Taken from our families and separated,

I know that your arguments is those were your ancestors,

Cannot understand why all of this has festered,

 Your only answer is. We should get over it!!

If that were your people Would you get over it?

 Black! Black! Black Lives Matters Black Lives Matter,

Black, Black! Black Lives Matter Black Lives Matter

Even after slavery y'all still make it hard,

Using your religion even changing God's,

Nationality like he came from ...,

While the bible clearly states somewhere near Jerusalem,

Your wealth was created on the backs of slaves,

Till u make it right there is nothing more to say,

We tried to be peaceful and we tried to kneel,

But every other day there is a black man killed,

And we ain't got nothing against the good police,

It is the bad police that need to cease,

The protests will stop when you treat us right!

Would you rather lose your city over equal rights?

Generational wealth is how you got your privilege,

Brain washed Africans with a tainted religion,

We believe in Jesus he was born in Bethlehem,

He either looks middle eastern or just like a black man!

Black! Black!

Black Lives Matters Black Lives Matter, Black! Black!

Black Lives Matter Black Lives Matter

We ain't overcome y'all,

Lord when you going to do it!

Before I will be a slave, I'll be buried in my grave

Photography Clay Banks

Photography Clay Banks

BLACK
LIVES
MATTER

HANDS UP, DON'T SHOOT

Hands up do not shoot,

Hands up do not shoot,

What u going to do when they come for you?

Hands up do not shoot, Hands up don't shoot,

We want equal rights! And to be treated like you.

Put your hands up, Put your hands down,

Turn around get down on the ground,

Any guns in the trunk tonight,

No officer just out here trying to fly a kite,

Heading to the park before the sun go down,

And I know your stopping me because my skin is brown, "

Well you are doing 20 in a 25!

And I would like to search your car if you really don't mind This a nice ride!

Who car is this?" "Is it yours? How can you afford this?

Where you work? Where you live? Who your mama is? Is you high?

Are you drunk? What it really is? What brings you to this side of town?

We are gentrified, and your skin is brown,

And I know that you are not headed over to Starbucks!

I see your black Bugatti and I said what the?"

Hands up do not shoot, Hands up don't shoot,

What u going to do when they come for you?

Hands up do not shoot, Hands up don't shoot,

We want equal rights! And to be treated like you.

Hands on my steering wheel, I am wondering if my dinner was last meal,

You are asking for my license and my registration,
This some Ole Jim Crowe type of a segregation,
You got the gun pointed at my head,
Telling me move wrong and your dead!
Now you got me face down on the ground,
All because my skin is brown!
Hands up do not shoot, Hands up don't shoot,
What u going to do when they come for you?
Hands up do not shoot, Hands up don't shoot,
We want equal rights! And to be treated like you.

Hands up do not shoot,
Hands up do not shoot,
What u going to do when they come for you?
Hands up do not shoot, Hands up don't shoot,
We want equal rights! And to be treated like you.

Photography by Koshu Kunii

Photography by Koshu Kunii

Photography by Clay Banks

REPARATIONS

4 million enslaved blood cries from the grave,

Sold like commodity, America's policy,

Killed like livestock,

Choked like the rooster cock,

Could not speak your language, Tortured with a 12- gauge!

Forced to pick cotton which bolstered your economy,

Alabama, Carolina, Georgia, Mississippi,

Arkansas, Texas, Florida, Tennessee,

Virginia Maryland Pass me the Hennessey!

48% of the GDP was created by people who look just like me!

New York City was birthed by the industry,

It is time for all y'all to kiss this pinky ring!

I want my 40 acres and a mule,

Y'all better have my money,

40 acres and a mule I am not trying to be funny, 4

0 acres and a mule Y'all owe us interest!

40 acres Torture, Slavery and Disrespect.

Instead of paying the slaves,

Y'all paid the slaveholders,

Reparations was a joke and you all know it!

Forced to eat slop and work all day,

That is why we have health conditions to this day,

Raped our women and u made us watch!

Then beat us with a whip called us belligerent,

Even had the nerve to call us a …

Truth is y'all were the ones that were ignorant,

Hung us from a tree if we ran away

When who in their right mind would want to stay?

Sold our children, never seen them again and you still do not see?

Where is your sin?

I want my, 40 acres and a mule,

Y'all better have my money,

40 acres and a mule I am not trying to be funny,

40 acres and a mule Y'all owe us interest!

40 acres Torture, Slavery and Disrespect.

And you refused to even let us learn to read!

Quick to crack a whip choke us make us bleed,

Twisted the bible to suit your evil try,

Calling us an animal when you are the one that's guilty,

There is only one God, there is only one Master,

Those that accepted him, the other ones are ......

Stop all the talk about supremacy,

You put your pants (on one leg at a time) just like me,

And your blood is red, I bet you would all be dead

I if you had to pick cotton all day and you was not fed!

If we treated, you like you treated us!

If you had to ride in the back seat of the bus! I think you know it! I know you will not show it!! I think you know it! I know you will not show it!!

I want my, 40 acres and a mule,

Y'all better have my money,

40 acres and a mule I am not trying to be funny,

40 acres and a mule Y'all owe us interest!

KAREN

Karen! Why you call the cops on me?

 Karen! Why can't you just let us be? Karen!

Why are you so afraid? Karen!

Why are you so full of hate?

Stepped in the park for some R&R,

Two slabs of ribs, When I seen 20 cop cars,

 Sitting at the pool trying to catch come rays,

When you ran up on me acting heck a strange,

Asking me if I live here,

Showed you my lease,

And you still had the nerve to call the police!

Selling bottle water in my neighborhood,

When you ran up on me said I wish you would,

Asking me if I have a permit!

Why are you so full of it?

Up in the park trying to watch some birds!

 When I hear a loud voice Saying excuse me sir!!

I do not understand why your filming me,

 Cause we all know you want to be with me,

I am going to call the cops and say you threatened me!

Stand for the anthem o say can you see!

I see you writing on the sidewalk, Black Lives Matter, it is time to talk!

Is this your house? I know you cannot afford it

I am going to call the cops,

Because I have just about had it!!

Sitting in my home watching the game!!

Broke down my door asking me my name,

Oooops!!

I am sorry wrong address! Shot by Karen. I Confess!!

Karen! Why you call the cops on me?

 Karen! Why can't you just let us be? Karen!

Why are you so afraid? Karen!

Why are you so full of hate?

Karen! Why you call the cops on me?

 Karen! Why can't you just let us be? Karen!

Why are you so afraid? Karen!

Why are you so full of hate?

7 MILLION LIGHT YEARS

"Well I see your face everywhere I go on the TV even at the picture show,

I think I seen her.

I am telling u I've seen her

And I just want to know if you want to go out this atmosphere

"Ooooh! Got me losing me cool,

 Cannot stop thinking about you girl,

Ooooh!! What am I supposed to?

do?

You got me feeling brand new... Girl

 I crash landed here do not really like it here,

 Folks do not know it, but I stand out from almost all my peers,

But you are the only one that stands out from humanity,

 You are not consumed by the riches and the vanity,

I think the worlds all aligned for me to crash upon your planet,

 I will never take this time with you for granted,

But it is for me to like it here,

All this hate and bigotry,

I was hoping deep inside that maybe you would come with me.

Ooooh! Got me losing me cool,

Cannot stop thinking about you girl,

Ooooh!! What am I supposed to do?

 You got me feeling brand new, Girl...

My planets far but we will both reside,

Here are my 16 bars once we die, we will be alive,

My spaceships almost fixed,

The engines almost ready,

I just need to hold you close and keep the throttle steady,

We need love for fuel,

We do not need no tools,

I just need to know if you feel the same way too.

We will travel to the nines,

Just give me a sign,

 And baby please don't let us this moment pass us by.

Ooooh! Got me losing me cool,

Can't stop thinking about you girl,

Ooooh!! What am I supposed to do?

 You got me feeling brand new, Girl...

The Coup De Grâce

Unite,

Africa!

Unite!

All my brothers and my sisters

UNITE!

Stand up and fight

UNITE!

Stop killing each other

UNITE!

This that battle cry, time 4 a drive-by

Y'all keep killing us, so do not ask why,

One more time we going to ask y'all to stop,

But if we see one more get killed by a cop it is on!

And when it is on, it is on!

Do not forget u heard it first in this song!

Buffalo soldiers ready and armed,

Vengeance from the Lord will be placed upon,

Those who trespass against humanity,

Time to bring sanity to this insanity,

The Lions of Africa,

Ready for war!
If you do not stop killing us, then it is on!

Africa stand up!! UNITE!

Unite,

Africa!

Unite,

All my brothers and my sisters

UNITE!

Stand up and fight

UNITE!

Stop killing each other

UNITE!

Calling all my black folk, Mexican and Puerto Rican,

Asians, Indians, Haitians and Dominicans,

Crips and bloods White folks and Africans,

All around the world from China to American,

The 3rd world war will be fought over color,

All my brothers stop killing my brothers,

Take up arms and take it to the man,

Sometimes violence is the only thing that they understand,

It is time for us to drive the bus,

You said to us in God you trust

Give us what ours or we just might take it,

Enslaving our people is what you hold sacred.

Unite,

Africa!

Unite,

All my brothers and my sisters

UNITE!

Stand up and fight

UNITE!

Stop killing each other

UNITE!

VOTE

Vote!

Everybody everywhere!

Vote!

Like your life depended on it!

Vote!

Time to let your voice be heard,

Photography Clay Banks

Make sure to buy the album available on all digital platforms!

Produced by Jenius

All music written, composed and arranged by Jenius

All lyrics written by Jenius

Piano: Jenius

Bass Guitar: Jenius

Lead Guitar: Jenius

Organ: Jenius

Keyboard Programming: Jenius

Acoustic Guitar: Jenius

Trumpet Horn Parts: Jenius

All Vocals: Jenius

Jerome Street

I was born in a town just outside Boston called West Medford a.k.a. "The Ville". West Medford and Medford were two totally different towns with a different racial and cultural identity. However, as a child I made friends with every nationality and did not even know anything about racism until I was about 8 years old. My parents were God fearing people who raised us to love everyone and treat everybody equally. My mother and father worked very hard to provide a good life for myself and my sister. Boston's educational foundation impacted my town as a child with an incredible amount of information regarding the arts, history and science. I started playing violin at age 7 and I loved going to school with all my friends. Boston is such a beautiful place to grow up and exist. This time period in my life was probably the best time in my life even to this day! I lived on Jerome street in a beautiful Victorian style home and there were plenty of children that I became friends with and enjoyed spending time riding bikes etc. I can still taste the maple flavored air and smell my favorite donuts being freshly prepared through the early morning walk to my childhood school Brooks Elementary. There was a store on the corner called Jack's where I would indulge myself with a morning hostess snack before I arrived at school each morning. We all walked together every day to ensure our safety and I was too young to walk alone so my sister Sharon always made sure I got to school safely. I attended a huge church called Concord Baptist when I was young, and I loved the fact that there were always a lot of children and activities. My family ended up becoming very close to quite a few people in the choir and even to this day consider them family. Daisy, Kevin, Jewel and Earl, Chasity, Monique, Erica and Joyce (last names kept private). Going to church meant a trip into the city and I always loved being in downtown Boston. My parents would always make the trip downtown very enjoyable by going shopping, eating at my favorite spots etc. Life was amazing in my hometown and I travel often back to my hometown as an adult just to walk the streets of my old neighborhood and enjoy the vibration. Boston had its own racial struggles, but they were so neatly tucked away that as a child you could hardly see the dynamics of how the racial divide played itself out. The cultures were basically divided into their own segregated sides of the city and I never even thought of it that way until later in life. I just remember all the great things about the food each culture brought to the table literally. Like I mentioned before I had friends of all nationalities and from almost every culture and I never felt like I was an outcast in this part of the country. Well everything was going great I loved my town and everything was awesome until one day I overheard my Aunt Daisy saying to my parents "Please don't move away we love you and this is a great place for the children etc." I did not know it, but my life was about to change in a very dramatic fashion. My parents decided to return to their hometown in Alabama to be closer to their parents who were aging and to assist them like good children. This was a very noble thing to do and I know my parents made the right decision for their lives and I respect their choice. So, with that said growing up near Boston and moving to Enterprise is like leaving Earth and traveling to another galaxy where you must learn the language, the culture the unspoken words and all the above. I tried to come to grips with my new town however "I came to realize that I wasn't in Kansas anymore" racial divides that plagued the Jim Crow south still existed and jumped out at me every chance it could get like a scary movie! Alabama was a beautiful place and if I had not grown up in Boston, I think I seriously would have loved the state. There were lots of cousins and activities however everything was different. I spoke like a true Bostonian, so I got picked on and made fun of daily. Since I spoke with an accent the kids would say I was a nerd. Children can be brutal, and this town did not hold back. I truly learned every aspect of racism during this time in my life and to many words to go into regarding this time period. Let's just say I got the memo! The church that I used to attend had been replaced with a much smaller church and it had a great music department, so I began to sing in the choir. The minister of music would have me sing a lot of lead parts since my voice was very high like Michael J when I was younger. I enjoyed the time I spent but it could never replace my church in Boston. The southern food that had been passed down from generation to generation was very foreign to me as well which made life very interesting in Alabama. I would often refuse to eat my dinner and I would not eat the southern foods many loved. Even the syrup was very different, and I was convinced I had been bamboozled. The fact that I had several cousins helped me tremendously with the change of location. I had one cousin to this day who is like a big brother my mother's brother son Cedric. If it had not been for my cousin Cedric, I think I would have run away back to Boston. Cedric was a football star in junior high who went on to become an NFL player and NFL coach. Cedric was always serious about his training and he also took a lot of time to make sure I had everything I needed .My other cousins were also very caring and made sure that nobody bothered me at all.(way too many too name) Also I had an incredible friend growing up who was into music as well and super talented he went on to become a preacher and is doing well for himself! We started recording and writing songs for our first band and at that point I realized I did not ever want to do anything other than music. We did not have a lot of equipment so we would use headphones as microphones and the way we overdubbed our tracks was with two large boom box radios lol. Sounds funny now but we wrote some hit songs during that time period. Great group of guys and incredibly talented!

 So, I guess family insulated me from the racism and hatred that was existing all around. As I started to get older, I quickly became aware of the fact that being a black person on earth can cost you your life. The schools in Boston taught the norths point of view regarding life which made you feel like you can be anything you want. The south's education reminded me very quickly that as a black man opportunity is not the same and to get used to the fact of how this is as a reality. So, I spent everyday planning on getting away from Alabama as soon as possible. I started learning the trumpet and piano and would dedicate my life to mastering these instruments as a way of escaping into a better life in the future. All my practicing paid off and I got a scholarship to go to a HBCU which was a cool and a great experience however I wanted to go to Berklee School of music. College life was a huge party and you must be grounded mentally to learn anything at all. There are many things to get into that can help you lose focus. I decided that I would like to join the military so I could get away with my own money and make my own decisions. So, I left college and joined the

Navy where I noticed a lot of dynamics. Racism exists in every part of American life you can read between the lines on this out of respect for the military. Anyway, I ended up getting a job in Washington DC working for the president and I was back in a metro area. I had never experienced being in a city that was predominantly black, and I loved my time in DC and learned a lot of very interesting things about life, music becoming an adult. I had family in Maryland, and they worked at the Pentagon, so life was starting to get good! I found myself trying to escape racism but, in every city, and every institution it was there and quick to say hello! This begins the start of being pulled over for driving while black! Since my military days I have been pulled over at least 79 times and I am not exaggerating in any way. I will not name states but let us just say all a whole lot! I got very experienced at being pulled over and learned how to get off without incident by handling the stops a certain way. Once they found out I worked for the President they would change their whole demeanor. In DC I was never stopped but nearby states lol let us just say they kicked it off in a major way. While I served in the military I also would sing in clubs and perform in talent contests etc. I got good at hiding the fact that I was an artist with my military friends and ranking officials. I had songs on the radio in the area and it was how I decided to use a different name for my music. Jenius/Gnyus After serving I decided to pursue music and I became quickly aware of how much racism exists in the music industry. You see, if you write about positive things a as black man you may never get any assistance. The companies love for you to write about women, drugs and money which helps perpetuate the way society is run. Thanks to the web artists can put their music and ideas out without record companies. I had three record contracts and they all went south when I would not write about sex drugs etc. Also, as a black artist who is classically trained as a musician you will lose your black fans when you start playing rock, classical pop etc. Also record companies do not push black artists who attempt to play rock. However, a few have escaped and made it into the genre lol. This book is about experiences that I have had firsthand and the experiences of black people all around the world. Many did not live to speak about these issues however I felt I had a responsibility to speak on the civil issues that plague many on this planet. Later I moved to Atlanta where I worked with record companies and many artists in the hip hop community who are household names to this day! I had friends go on to write Grammy nominated songs which are classic hits today. I was put in a position to meet almost everyone you can think of in the music industry (too many too name.) I was signed to a small record label and out of loyalty never approached some of the musical giants I had the pleasure of hanging out with at the time. Any major artists from New York to Atlanta I have just about met and broke bread. I noticed at the time that it was very important for record labels to sign black artists in only certain genres. Hip Hop became the saving grace because it allowed us to do whatever we wanted as artists. I also had two different opportunities that were dealing with Prince. The first was a group of incredible artists out of Smyrna Georgia called Van Gogh. Prince gave them a song and I had the pleasure of playing on some of the songs on that record.

The guys in Van Gogh outworked any musicians I know and are incredible!

Check out this link for more information
https://www.youtube.com/watch?v=eXXnLc8ZZ4E

The second round with Prince was in California where I was hanging with local musicians who all ended up being princes band wow!

I missed out on this opportunity for numerous reasons

it is important to be vigilant in your life

you never know if you do not keep a watchful eye, I was on a plane back to Atlanta when my destiny was in California great learning lesson in life.

Check out the musicians here

https://www.youtube.com/watch?v=lElCzhjiPX8

Atlanta was very similar to DC in many ways and had a huge amount of racial challenges just outside the city limit! Next up got a singing job in South Korea playing on the military bases this is where I got my live performance together. This is also when I realized that my people are hated on all four corners of the globe. Like America there are many Koreans who were so nice and then you had the ones like everywhere you go as a black man .Great learning experience and I have to say the Koreans are a very beautiful people and they have an amazing history and culture! In many ways the Koreans endured some of the same issues as my fellow black Americans, so we have much more in common just take a glimpse into their history. So up next was Europe which got cut short when America went to war, and we came back to the states. I returned to the states looking to stay active as a musician and eventually found a lead position singing in South Carolina which embodied all racial aspects fully lol. I was singing Guns and Roses, Bon Jovi, and Metallica to a majority non diverse crowd of patrons who accepted this well given the context and situation. Then I would turn around and cover some of the most popular rap songs on the radio. I learned a great deal about people, and I am certain that many patrons learned a great deal from me. I left this band and moved to Charlotte Nc where there is a lot of dynamics lol. During this time, I attempted to live a normal life with a regular job had an amazing son K'von! Music called me back and I answered by working with James Brown's family and then returned back to South Carolina where I rejoined the band I left who changed their name with the same people and came back as a piano player. I would sing a few songs but not the same as before. I enjoyed Myrtle Beach and went on to have a beautiful daughter Anastasia! Both of my children have several gifts and it will be very interesting to see how they express their talent!! I met many great people in South Carolina both black and white, Asian and Hispanic. It appears that racism can be dealt with once people realize that we are all human beings! This is not a book to further division, but it is a realistic look at the past present and what a future could look like! The lyrics are a description of what happened to my ancestors and I know it may be hard to hear However this is probably the first time in history where there is enough people standing up for justice in all cultures! Love is more powerful than hate and I plead with you to put down your arms and join the rest of humanity! One Love!

To all my friends I love you no matter where you are from in this world!

It was hard to write this book because I did not want to offend anyone.

I have had great white friends who literally invested in my life and would have given the shirt off their own backs.

It is important to me to not hurt anyone however at the same time,

If speaking of the pain I and my ancestors went through bother you perhaps.......

DO NOT FORGET

David McAtee, August 3, 1966 - June 1, 2020 Louisville, Kentucky Shot: June 1, 2020, Louisville Metropolitan Police Officer George Perry Floyd, October 14, 1973 - May 25, 2020 Powder horn, Minneapolis, Minnesota Knee on neck/Asphyxiated: May 25, 2020, Minneapolis Police Officer Dreasjon "Sean" Reed, 1999 - May 6, 2020 Indianapolis, Indiana Shot: May 6, 2020, Unidentified Indianapolis Metropolitan Police Officer Michael Brent Charles Ramos, January 1, 1978 - April 24, 2020 Austin, Texas Shot: April 24, 2020, Austin Police Detectives Breonna Taylor, June 5, 1993 - March 13, 2020 Louisville, Kentucky Shot: March 13, 2020, Louisville Metro Police Officers Manuel "Mannie" Elijah Ellis, August 28, 1986 - March 3, 2020 Tacoma, Washington Physical restraint/Hypoxia: March 3, 2020, Tacoma Police Officers WOKE 30 Atatiana Koquice Jefferson, November 28, 1990 - October 12, 2019 Fort Worth, Texas Shot: October 12, 2019, Fort Worth Police Officer Emantic "EJ" Fitzgerald Bradford Jr., June 18, 1997 - November 22, 2018 Hoover, Alabama Shot: November 22, 2018, Unidentified Hoover Police Officers Charles "Chop" Roundtree Jr., September 5, 2000 - October 17, 2018 San Antonio, Texas Shot: October 17, 2018, San Antonio Police Officer Chinedu Okobi, February 13, 1982 - October 3, 2018 Millbrae, California Tasered/Electrocuted: October 3, 2018, San Mateo County Sheriff Sergeant and Sheriff Deputies Botham Shem Jean, September 29, 1991 - September 6, 2018 Dallas, Texas Shot: September 6, 2018, Dallas Police Officer Antwon Rose Jr., July 12, 2000 - June 19, 2018 East Pittsburgh, Pennsylvania Shot: June 19, 2018, East Pittsburgh Police Officer Saheed Vassell, December 22, 1983 - April 4, 2018 Brooklyn, New York City, New York Shot: April 4, 2018, Four Unnamed New York City Police Officers Stephon Alonzo Clark, August 10, 1995 - March 18, 2018 Sacramento, California Shot: March 18, 2018, Sacramento Police Officers Aaron Bailey, 1972 - June 29, 2017 Indianapolis, Indiana Shot: June 29, 2017, Indianapolis Metropolitan Police Officers Charleena Chavon Lyles, April 24, 1987 - June 18, 2017 Seattle, Washington Shot: June 18, 2017, Seattle Police Officers Fetus of Charleena Chavon Lyles (14-15 weeks), June 18, 2017 Seattle, Washington Shot: June 18, 2017, Seattle Police Officers Jordan Edwards, October 25, 2001 - April 29, 2017 Balch Springs, Texas Shot: April 29, 2017, Balch Springs Officer WOKE 32 Chad Robertson, 1992 - February 15, 2017 Chicago, Illinois Shot: February 8, 2017, Chicago Police Officer Deborah Danner, September 25, 1950 - October 18, 2016 The Bronx, New York City, New York Shot: October 18, 2016, New York City Police Officers Alfred Olango, July 29, 1978 - September 27, 2016 El Cajon, California Shot: September 27, 2016, El Cajon Police Officers Terence Crutcher, August 16, 1976 - September 16, 2016 Tulsa, Oklahoma Shot: September 16, 2016, Tulsa Police Officer Terrence LeDell Sterling, July 31, 1985 - September 11, 2016 Washington, DC Shot: September 11, 2016, Washington Metropolitan Police Officer Korryn Gaines, August 24, 1993 - August 1, 2016 Randallstown, Maryland Shot: August 1, 2016, Baltimore County Police WOKE 33 Joseph Curtis Mann, 1966 - July 11, 2016 Sacramento, California Shot: July 11, 2016, Sacramento Police Officers Philando Castile, July 16, 1983 - July 6, 2016

Falcon Heights, Minnesota Shot: July 6, 2016, St. Anthony Police Officer Alton Sterling, June 14, 1979 - July 5, 2016 Baton Rouge, Louisiana Shot: July 5, 2016, Baton Rouge Police Officers Bettie "Betty Boo" Jones, 1960 - December 26, 2015 Chicago, Illinois Shot: December 26, 2015, Chicago Police Officer Quintonio LeGrier, April 29, 1996 - December 26, 2015 Chicago, Illinois Shot: December 26, 2015, Chicago Police Officer Corey Lamar Jones, February 3, 1984 - October 18, 2015 Palm Beach Gardens, Florida Shot: October 18, 2015, Palm Beach Gardens Police Officer WOKE 34 Jamar O'Neal Clark, May 3, 1991 - November 16, 2015 Minneapolis, Minnesota Shot: November 15, 2015, Minneapolis Police Officers Jeremy "Bam Bam" McDole, 1987 - September 23, 2015 Wilmington, Delaware Shot: September 23, 2015, Wilmington Police Officers India Kager, June 9, 1988 - September 5, 2015 Virginia Beach, Virginia Shot: September 5, 2015, Virginia Beach Police Officers Samuel Vincent DuBose, March 12, 1972 - July 19, 2015 Cincinnati, Ohio Shot: July 19, 2015, University of Cincinnati Police Officer Sandra Bland, February 7, 1987 - July 13, 2015 Waller County, Texas Excessive Force/Wrongful Death/Suicide (?): July 10, 2015, Texas State Trooper Brendon K. Glenn, 1986 - May 5, 2015 Venice, California Shot: May 5, 2015, Los Angeles Police Officer Freddie Carlos Gray Jr., August 16, 1989 - April 19, 2015 Baltimore, Maryland Brute Force/Spinal Injuries: April 12, 2015, Baltimore City Police Officers Walter Lamar Scott, February 9, 1965 - April 4, 2015 North Charleston, South Carolina Shot: April 4, 2015, North Charleston Police Officer Eric Courtney Harris, October 10, 1971 - April 2, 2015 Tulsa, Oklahoma Shot: April 2, 2015, Tulsa County Reserve Deputy Phillip Gregory White, 1982 - March 31, 2015 Vineland, New Jersey K-9 Mauling/Respiratory distress: March 31, 2015, Vineland Police Officers Mya Shawatza Hall, December 5, 1987 - March 30, 2015 Fort Meade, Maryland Shot: March 30, 2015, National Security Agency Police Officers Meagan Hockaday, August 27, 1988 - March 28, 2015 Oxnard, California Shot: March 28, 2015, Oxnard Police Officer WOKE 36 Tony Terrell Robinson, Jr., October 18, 1995 - March 6, 2015 Madison, Wisconsin Shot: March 6, 2015, Madison Police Officer Janisha Fonville, March 3, 1994 - February 18 2015 Charlotte, North Carolina Shot: February 18, 2015, Charlotte-Mecklenburg Police Officer Natasha McKenna, January 9, 1978 - February 8, 2015 Fairfax County, Virginia Tasered/Cardiac Arrest: February 3, 2015, Fairfax County Sheriff Deputies Jerame C. Reid, June 8, 1978 - December 30, 2014 Bridgeton, New Jersey Shot: December 30, 2014, Bridgeton Police Officer Rumain Brisbon, November 24, 1980 - December 2, 2014 Phoenix, Arizona Shot: December 2, 2014, Phoenix Police Officer Tamir Rice, June 15, 2002 - November 22, 2014 Cleveland, Ohio Shot: November 22, 2014, Cleveland Police Officer WOKE 37 Akai Kareem Gurley, November 12, 1986 - November 20, 2014 Brooklyn, New York City, New York Shot: November 20, 2014, New York City Police Officer Tanisha N. Anderson, January 22, 1977 - November 13, 2014 Cleveland, Ohio Physically Restrained/Brute Force: November 13, 2014, Cleveland Police Officers Dante Parker, August 14, 1977 - August 12, 2014 Victorville, California Tasered/Excessive Force: August 12, 2014, San Bernardino County Sheriff Deputies Ezell Ford, October 14, 1988 - August 11, 2014 Florence, Los Angeles, California Shot: August 11, 2014, Los Angeles Police Officers Michael Brown Jr., May 20, 1996 - August 9, 2014 Ferguson, Missouri Shot: August 9, 2014, Ferguson Police Officer John Crawford III, July 29, 1992 - August 5, 2014 Beavercreek, Ohio Shot: August 5, 2014, Beavercreek Police

Officer WOKE 38 Eric Garner, September 15, 1970 - July 17, 2014 Staten Island, New York Choke hold/Suffocated: July 17, 2014, New York City Police Officer Dontre Hamilton, January 20, 1983 - April 30, 2014 Milwaukee, Wisconsin Shot: April 30, 2014, Milwaukee Police Officer Victor White III, September 11, 1991 - March 3, 2014 New Iberia, Louisiana Shot: March 2, 2014, Iberia Parish Sheriff Deputy Gabriella Monique Nevarez, November 25, 1991 - March 2, 2014 Citrus Heights, California Shot: March 2, 2014, Citrus Heights Police Officers Yvette Smith, December 18, 1966 - February 16, 2014 Bastrop County, Texas Shot: February 16, 2014, Bastrop County Sheriff Deputy McKenzie J. Cochran, August 25, 1988 - January 29, 2014 Southfield, Michigan Pepper Sprayed/Compression Asphyxiation: January 28, 2014, Northland Mall Security Guards WOKE 39 Jordan Baker, 1988 - January 16, 2014 Houston, Texas Shot: January 16, 2014, Off-duty Houston Police Officer Andy Lopez, June 2, 2000 - October 22, 2013 Santa Rosa, California Shot: October 22, 2013, Sonoma County Sheriff Deputy Miriam Iris Carey, August 12, 1979 - October 3, 2013 Washington, DC Shot 26 times: October 3, 2013, U. S. Secret Service Officer Barrington "BJ" Williams, 1988 - September 17, 2013 New York City, New York Neglect/Disdain/Asthma Attack: September 17, 2013, New York City Police Officers Jonathan Ferrell, October 11, 1989 - September 14, 2013 Charlotte, North Carolina Shot: September 14, 2013, Charlotte-Mecklenburg Police Officer Carlos Alcis, 1970 - August 15, 2013 Brooklyn, New York City Heart Attack/Neglect: August 15, 2013, New York City Police Officers WOKE 40 Larry Eugene Jackson Jr., November 29, 1980 - July 26, 2013 Austin, Texas Shot: July 26, 2013, Austin Police Detective Kyam Livingston, July 29, 1975 - July 21, 2013 New York City, New York Neglect/Ignored pleas for help: July 20-21, 2013, New York City Police Officers Clinton R. Allen, September 26, 1987 - March 10, 2013 Dallas, Texas Tasered and Shot: March 10, 2013, Dallas Police Officer Kimani "KiKi" Gray, October 19, 1996 - March 9, 2013 Brooklyn, New York City, New York Shot: March 9, 2013, New York Police Officers Kayla Moore, April 17, 1971 - February 13, 2013 Berkeley, California Restrained face-down prone: February 12, 2013, Berkeley Police Officers Jamaal Moore Sr., 1989 - December 15, 2012 Chicago, Illinois Shot: December 15, 2012, Chicago Police Officer WOKE 41 Johnnie Kamahi Warren, February 26, 1968 - February 13, 2012 Dothan, Alabama Tasered/Electrocuted: December 10, 2012, Houston County (AL) Sheriff Deputy Shelly Marie Frey, April 21, 1985 - December 6, 2012 Houston, Texas Shot: December 6, 2012, Off-duty Harris County Sheriff's Deputy Darnisha Diana Harris, December 11, 1996 - December 2, 2012 Breaux Bridge, Louisiana Shot: December 2, 2012, Breaux Bridge Police Officer Timothy Russell, December 9. 1968 - November 29, 2012 Cleveland, Ohio 137 Rounds/Shot 23 times: November 29, 2012, Cleveland Police Officers Malissa Williams, June 20, 1982 - November 29, 2012 Cleveland, Ohio 137 Rounds/Shot 24 times: November 29, 2012, Cleveland Police Officers Noel Palanco, November 28, 1989 - October 4, 2012 Queens, New York City, New York Shot: October 4, 2012, New York City Police Officers WOKE 42 Reynaldo Cuevas, January 6, 1992 - September 7, 2012 Bronx, New York City, New York Shot: September 7, 2012, New York City Police Officer Chavis Carter, 1991 - July 28, 2012 Jonesboro, Arkansas Shot: July 28, 2012, Jonesboro Police Officer Alesia Thomas, June 1, 1977 - July 22, 2012 Los Angeles, California Brutal Force/Beaten: July 22, 2012, Los Angeles Police Officers Shantel Davis, May 26, 1989 - June 14, 2012 New

York City, New York Shot: June 14, 2012, New York City Police Officer Sharmel T. Edwards, October 10, 1962 - April 21, 2012 Las Vegas, Nevada Shot: April 21, 2012, Las Vegas Police Officers Tamon Robinson, December 21, 1985 - April 18, 2012 Brooklyn, New York City, New York Run over by police car: April 12, 2012, New York City Police Officers Ervin Lee Jefferson, III, 1994 - March 24, 2012 Atlanta, Georgia WOKE 43 Shot: March 24, 2012, Shepperson Security & Escort Services Security Guards Kendrec McDade, May 5, 1992 - March 24, 2012 Pasadena, California Shot: March 24, 2012, Pasadena Police Officers Rekia Boyd, November 5, 1989 - March 21, 2012 Chicago, Illinois Shot: March 21, 2012, Off-duty Chicago Police Detective Shereese Francis, 1982 - March 15, 2012 Queens, New York City, New York Suffocated to death: March 15, 2012, New York City Police Officers Jersey K. Green, June 17, 1974 - March 12, 2012 Aurora, Illinois Tasered/Electrocuted: March 12, 2012, Aurora Police Officers Wendell James Allen, December 19, 1991 - March 7, 2012 New Orleans, Louisiana Shot: March 7, 2012, New Orleans Police Officer Nehemiah Lazar Dillard, July 29, 1982 - March 5, 2012 Gainesville, Florida WOKE 44 Tasered/Electrocuted: March 5, 2012, Alachua County Sheriff Deputies Dante' Lamar Price, July 18, 1986 - March 1, 2012 Dayton, Ohio Shot: March 1, 2012, Ranger Security Guards Raymond Luther Allen Jr., 1978 - February 29, 2012 Galveston, Texas Tasered/Electrocuted: February 27, 2012, Galveston Police Officers Manual Levi Loggins Jr., February 22, 1980 - February 7, 2012 San Clemente, Orange County, California Shot: February 7, 2012, Orange County Sheriff Deputy Ramarley Graham, April 12, 1993 - February 2, 2012 The Bronx, New York City, New York Shot: February 2, 2012, New York City Police Officer Kenneth Chamberlain Sr., April 12, 1943 - November 19, 2011 White Plains, New York Tasered/Electrocuted/Shot: November 19, 2011, White Plains Police Officers WOKE 45 Alonzo Ashley, June 10, 1982 - July 18, 2011 Denver, Colorado Tasered/Electrocuted: July 18, 2011, Denver Police Officers Derek Williams, January 23, 1989 - July 6, 2011 Milwaukee, Wisconsin Blunt Force/Respiratory distress: July 6, 2011, Milwaukee Police Officers Raheim Brown, Jr., March 4, 1990 - January 22, 2011 Oakland, California Shot: January 22, 2011, Oakland Unified School District Police Reginald Doucet, June 3, 1985 - January 14, 2011 Los Angeles, California Shot: January 14, 2011, Los Angeles Police Officer Derrick Jones, September 30, 1973 - November 8, 2010 Oakland, California Shot: November 8, 2010, Oakland Police Officers Danroy "DJ" Henry Jr., October 29, 1990 - October 17, 2010 Pleasantville, New York Shot: October 17, 2020, Pleasantville Police Officer WOKE 46 Aiyana Mo'Nay Stanley-Jones, July 20, 2002 - May 16, 2010 Detroit, Michigan Shot: May 16, 2010, Detroit Police Officer Steven Eugene Washington, September 20, 1982 - March 20, 2010 Los Angeles, California Shot: March 20, 2010, Los Angeles County Police Aaron Campbell, September 7, 1984 - January 29, 2010 Portland, Oregon Shot: January 29, 2010, Portland Police Officer Kiwane Carrington, July 14, 1994 - October 9, 2009 Champaign, Illinois Shot: October 9, 2019, Champaign Police Officer Victor Steen, November 11, 1991 - October 3, 2009 Pensacola, Florida Tasered/Run over: October 3, 2009, Pensacola Police Officer Shem Walker, March 18, 1960 - July 11, 2009 Brooklyn, New York Shot: July 11, 2009, New York City Undercover C-94 Police Officer WOKE 47 Oscar Grant III, February 27, 1986 - January 1, 2009 Oakland, California Shot: January 1, 2009, BART Police Officer Tarika Wilson, October 30, 1981 - January 4, 2008 Lima, Ohio Shot January 4, 2008,

Lima Police Officer DeAunta Terrel Farrow, September 7, 1994 - June 22, 2007 West Memphis, Arkansas Shot: June 22, 2007, West Memphis (AR) Police Officer Sean Bell, May 23, 1983 - November 25, 2006 Queens, New York City, New York Shot: November 25, 2006, New York City Police Officers Kathryn Johnston, June 26, 1914 - November 21, 2006 Atlanta, Georgia Shot: November 21, 2006, Undercover Atlanta Police Officers Ronald Curtis Madison, March 1, 1965 - September 4, 2005 Danziger Bridge, New Orleans, Louisiana Shot: September 4, 2005, New Orleans Police Officers WOKE 48 James B. Brissette Jr., November 6, 1987 - September 4, 2005 Danziger Bridge, New Orleans, Louisiana Shot: September 4, 2005, New Orleans Police Officers Henry "Ace" Glover, October 2, 1973 - September 2, 2005 New Orleans, Louisiana Shot: September 2, 2005, New Orleans Police Officers Timothy Stansbury, Jr., November 16, 1984 - January 24, 2004 Brooklyn, New York City, New York Shot: January 24, 2004, New York City Police Officer Ousmane Zongo, 1960 - May 22, 2003 New York City, New York Shot: May 22, 2003, New York City Police Officer Alberta Spruill, 1946 - May 16, 2003 New York City, New York Stun grenade thrown into her apartment led to a heart attack: May 16, 2003, New York City Police Officer Kendra Sarie James, December 24, 1981 - May 5, 2003 Portland, Oregon Shot: May 5, 2003, Portland Police Officer WOKE 49 Orlando Barlow, December 29, 1974 - February 28, 2003 Las Vegas, Nevada Shot: February 28, 2003, Las Vegas Police Officer Timothy DeWayne Thomas Jr., July 25, 1981 - April 7, 2001 Cincinnati, Ohio Shot: April 7, 2001, Cincinnati Police Patrolman Ronald Beasley, 1964 - June 12, 2000 Dellwood, Missouri Shot: June 12, 2000, Dellwood Police Officers Earl Murray, 1964 - June 12, 2000 Dellwood, Missouri Shot: June 12, 2000, Dellwood Police Officers Patrick Moses Dorismond, February 28, 1974 - March 16, 2000 New York City, New York Shot: March 16, 2000, New York City Police Officer Prince Carmen Jones Jr., March 30, 1975 - September 1, 2000 Fairfax County, Virginia Shot: September 1, 2000, Prince George's County Police Officer WOKE 50 Malcolm Ferguson, October 31, 1976 - March 1, 2000 The Bronx, New York City, New York Shot: March 1, 2000, New York City Police Officer LaTanya Haggerty, 1973 - June 4, 1999 Chicago, Illinois Shot: June 4, 1999, Chicago Police Officer Margaret LaVerne Mitchell, 1945 - May 21, 1999 Los Angeles, California Shot: May 21, 1999, Los Angeles Police Officer Amadou Diallo, September 2, 1975 - February 4, 1999 The Bronx, New York City, New York Shot: February 4, 1999, New York City Police Officers Tyisha Shenee Miller, March 9, 1979 - December 28, 1998 Riverside, California Shot: December 28, 1998, Riverside Police Officers Dannette Daniels, January 25, 1966 - June 7, 1997 Newark, New Jersey Shot: June 7, 1997, Newark Police Officer WOKE 51 Frankie Ann Perkins, 1960 - March 22, 1997 Chicago, Illinois Brutal Force/Strangled: March 22, 1997, Chicago Police Officers Nicholas Heyward Jr., August 26, 1981 - September 27, 1994 Brooklyn, New York City, New York Shot: September 27, 1994, New York City Police Officer Mary Mitchell, 1950 - November 3, 1991 The Bronx, New York City, New York Shot: November 3, 1991, New York City Police Officer Yvonne Smallwood, 1959 - December 9, 1987 New York City, New York Severely beaten/Massive blood clot: December 3, New York City Police Officers Eleanor Bumpers, August 22, 1918 - October 29, 1984 The Bronx, New York City, New York Shot: October 29, 1984, New York City Police Officer Michael Jerome Stewart, May 9, 1958 - September 28, 1983 New York City, New York Brutal Force: September 15, 1983, New York City Transit Police WOKE 52

Eula Mae Love, August 8, 1939 - January 3, 1979 Los Angeles, California Shot: January 3, 1979, Los Angeles County Police Officers Arthur Miller Jr., 1943 - June 14, 1978 Brooklyn, New York City, New York Chokehold/Strangled: June 14, 1978, New York City Police Officers Randolph Evans, April 5, 1961 - November 25, 1976 Brooklyn, New York City, New York Shot in head: November 25, 1976, New York City Police Officer Barry Gene Evans, August 29, 1958 - February 10, 1976 Los Angeles, California Shot: February 10, 1976, Los Angeles Police Officers Rita Lloyd, January 27, 1973 New York City, New York Shot: January 27, 1973, New York City Police Officer Henry Dumas, July 20, 1934 - May 23, 1968 Harlem, New York City, New York Shot: May 23, 1968, New York City Transit Police Officer

Photo

graphy by Clay Banks

Over the period of the Atlantic Slave Trade, from approximately 1526 to 1867, some 12.5 million slaves had been shipped from Africa, and 10.7 million had arrived in the Americas. The Atlantic Slave Trade was likely the costliest in human life of all of long-distance global migrations. The first Africans forced to work in the New World left from Europe at the beginning of the sixteenth century, not from Africa. The first slave voyage direct from Africa to the Americas probably sailed in 1526. The volume of slaves carried off from Africa reached thirty thousand per year in the 1690s and eighty-five thousand per year a century later. More than eight out of ten Africans forced into the slave trade made their journeys in the century and a half after 1700. By 1820, nearly four Africans for every one European had crossed the Atlantic. About four out of every five females that traversed the Atlantic were from Africa. The majority of enslaved Africans were brought to British North America between 1720 and 1780. The decade 1821 to 1830 still saw over 80,000 people a year leaving Africa in slave ships. Well over a million more – one tenth of the volume carried off in the slave trade era – followed within the next twenty years. Africans carried to Brazil came overwhelmingly from Angola. Africans carried to North America, including the Caribbean, left from mainly West Africa. WOKE 54 Well over 90 percent of enslaved Africans were imported into the Caribbean and South America. Only about 6 percent of African captives were sent directly to British North America. Yet by 1825, the US had a quarter of blacks in the New World. The Middle Passage was dangerous and miserable for African slaves. The sexes were separated, kept naked, packed close together, and the men were chained for long periods. About twelve percent of those who embarked did not survive the voyage. US SLAVERY COMPARED TO SLAVERY IN THE AMERICAS American plantations were dwarfed by those in the West Indies. In the Caribbean, slaves were held on much larger units, with many plantations holding 150 slaves or more. In the American South, in contrast, only one slaveholder held as many as a thousand slaves, and just 125 had over 250 slaves. In the Caribbean, Dutch Guiana, and Brazil, the slave death rate was so high and the birth rate so low that they could not sustain their population without importations from Africa. Rates of natural decrease ran as high as 5 percent a year. While the death rate of US slaves was about the same as that of Jamaican slaves, the fertility rate was more than 80 percent higher in the United States. US slaves were more generations removed from Africa than those in the Caribbean. In the nineteenth century, most slaves in the British Caribbean and Brazil were born in Africa. In contrast, by 1850, most US slaves were third-, fourth-, or fifth generation Americans. Slavery in the US was distinctive in the near balance of the sexes and the ability of the slave population to increase its numbers by natural reproduction. Unlike any other slave society, the US had a high and sustained natural increase in the slave population for a more than a century and a half. CHILDREN There were few instances in which slave women were released from field work for extended periods during slavery. Even during the last week before childbirth, pregnant women on average picked three-quarters or more of the amount normal for women. Infant and child mortality rates were twice as high among slave children as among southern white children. Half of all slave infants died in their first year of life. A major contributor to the high infant and child death rate was chronic undernourishment. The average birth weight of slave infants was less than 5.5 pounds, considered severely underweight by today's standards. Most infants of enslaved mothers were weaned within three or four months. Even in the eighteenth century, the earliest weaning age advised by doctors was eight months. WOKE 56 After weaning, slave infants were fed a starch-based diet, consisting of foods such as gruel, which lacked sufficient nutrients for health and growth. HEALTH AND MORTALITY Slaves suffered a variety of miserable and often fatal maladies due to the Atlantic Slave Trade, and to inhumane living and working conditions. Common symptoms among enslaved populations included: blindness; abdominal swelling; bowed legs; skin lesions; and convulsions. Common conditions among enslaved populations included: beriberi (caused by a deficiency of thiamine); pellagra (caused by a niacin deficiency); tetany (caused by deficiencies of calcium, magnesium, and Vitamin D); rickets (also caused by a deficiency of Vitamin D); and kwashiorkor (caused by severe protein deficiency). Diarrhea, dysentery, whooping cough, and respiratory diseases as well as worms pushed the infant and early childhood death rate of slaves to twice that experienced by white infants and children. DOMESTIC SLAVE TRADE The domestic slave trade in the US distributed the African American population throughout the South in a migration that greatly surpassed in volume the Atlantic Slave Trade to North America. WOKE 57 Though Congress outlawed the African slave trade in 1808, domestic slave trade flourished, and the slave population in the US nearly tripled over the next 50 years. The domestic trade continued into the

1860s and displaced approximately 1.2 million men, women, and children, the vast majority of whom were born in America. To be "sold down the river" was one of the most dreaded prospects of the enslaved population. Some destinations, particularly the Louisiana sugar plantations, had especially grim reputations. But it was the destruction of family that made the domestic slave trade so terrifying. PROFITABILITY Prices of slaves varied widely over time, due to factors including supply, and changes in prices of commodities such as cotton. Even considering the relative expense of owning and keeping a slave, slavery was profitable. In order to ensure the profitability of slaves, and to produce maximum "return on investment," slave owners generally supplied only the minimum food and shelter needed for survival and forced their slaves to work from sunrise to sunset. Although young adult men had the highest expected levels of output, young adult women had value over and above their ability to work in the fields; they were able to have children who by law were also slaves of the owner of the mother. Therefore, the average price of female slaves was WOKE 58 higher than their male counterparts up to puberty age. Men around the age of 25-years-old were the most "valuable." Slaveholding became more concentrated over time, particularly as slavery was abolished in the northern states. The fraction of households owning slaves fell from 36 percent in 1830 to 25 percent in 1860. During the Civil War, roughly 180,000 black men served in the Union Army, and another 29,000 served in the Navy. Three-fifths of all black troops were former slaves. WORKS CITED AND RESOURCES University of Virginia, American Slave Narratives the Trans-Atlantic Slave Trade Database, Emory University the Interesting Narrative of the Life of Olaudah Equiano, Or Gustavus Vassa, The African (1789) Special thanks to Steven Mintz, University of Texas

Jenius

BLACK
LIVES
MATTER
SILENCE
IS
COMPLICITY

Noah Pederson

Photo by Jakayla Toney

Photo by Max Bender

Photo by Teemu Paananen

SAY THEIR
NAMES

IF YOU'RE NOT ANGRY, THEN YOU'RE NOT LISTENING.
Black LIVES MATTER
JUSTIC
EAC

Rach

ael Henning

DADDY LOVES YOU

Cali Records (c) 2020
Produced by L.M. Blair
Music by L.M. Blair
Lyrics by Jenius

When this world gets you down, I will always be around,
Just remember that Daddy Loves You!!
No matter come what may,
If I am far away just remember that
Daddy Loves You
You are my heart and soul I want you to know you are more than valuable,
Daddy Loves You
I think about you every single day,
I just want to say Daddy Loves You!!

1. Sometimes I know you look around and ask where is daddy at?
It must be hard to comprehend without all the facts
See sometimes people fall in love and then it falls apart,
But Anastasia and K'von you will always have my heart!!
I know you might be kind of mad about the way things are
It is important that you understand that you are my star!!!!!
I am working hard to try and make a better life for you
So, you can grow up find your purpose maybe go to school,
Sometimes situations in this world are out of our control,
And as you grow up you will see this world can be so cold,
Do not let the coldness of this world put your fire out,
And always focus on the positive and not the doubt!
I love you both with all my heart body and my soul,
And when you get to feeling bad, I want you both to know,
Can't nobody in this world ever take your place
I love you both Anastasia and K'von Grace......

When this world gets you down, I will always be around,
Just remember that Daddy Loves You!!
No matter come what may,
If I am far away just remember that
Daddy Loves You
You are my heart and soul I want you to know you are more than valuable,
Daddy Loves You

I think about you every single day,
I just want to say Daddy Loves You!!

 I am not perfect never met nobody else who is
As you grow up in this world do not forget to live,
And if you seem someone that's struggling its ok to give,
Never treat nobody badly cause the color of their skin,
Always do your best and be a good boy and girl,
Just remember that I am blessed to have you in my world,
As you get older you will understand a little more,
Wisdom versus education are two different doors,
Be respectful to your mommy and your daddy too,
Just remember that we both love you
Be respectful to your mommy and your daddy too
And remember that Your Daddy Loves You!!

When this world gets you down, I will always be around,
Just remember that Daddy Loves You!!
No matter come what may,
If I am far away just remember that
Daddy Loves You
You are my heart and soul I want you to know you are more than valuable,
Daddy Loves You
I think about you every single day,
I just want to say Daddy Loves You!!

 You will make a lot of friends but also enemies
Just be grateful for them both I call them frenemies,
They have a purpose in your life some are good, and some are bad,
You got a momma in this world you also got a Dad!
You are created out of love and you are a miracle,
You are both the creme of the crop that is the pinnacle!
I would die for you both that is how much I love you
I never loved before until the day I met you!!!

When this world gets you down, I will always be around,
Just remember that Daddy Loves You!!
No matter come what may,
If I am far away just remember that
Daddy Loves You
You are my heart and soul I want you to know you are more than valuable,
Daddy Loves You
I think about you every single day,
I just want to say Daddy Loves You!!

Cali Records (c) 2020
Produced by L.M. Blair

Music by L.M. Blair
Lyrics by Jenius

JENIUS

THE PROPHECY

I CAN SEE THE PROPHECY,

I CAN SEE THE FUTURE AND WHAT IT ALL WILL BE,

LISTEN TO THIS PROPHECY

CAUSE IF THERE IS NO UNITY,

THEN THERE IS NO YOU AND ME...

SAID I'M CALLING ALL HUMANITY,

EVERY COLOR,

ETHNIC GROUP AND CREED,

IT IS TIME TO LET LOVE SUPERCEDE,

ALL THE HATRED AND THE BIGOTRY,

SAID WE GOTTA GET TOGETHER YALL,

OR THE HUMAN RACE SHALL SURELY FALL,

SEE THE PERSON THAT YOUR PUTTING DOWN,

IS THE PERSON THAT WILL WEAR A CROWN!

I CAN SEE THE PROPHECY,

I CAN SEE THE FUTURE AND WHAT IT ALL WILL BE,

LISTEN TO THIS PROPHECY

CAUSE IF THERE IS NO UNITY,
THEN THERE IS NO YOU AND ME...

YOU SEE THERE IS ONLY ONE KING,
AND HE IS LORD OVER EVERYTHING,
EVERY SICKNESS, ILLNESS AND DISEASE,
HAS BEEN CAUSED BY OUR INIQUITY,
THERE IS NO MAN BETTER THAN ANOTHER,
WE ARE FATHERS MOTHERS SISTERS BROTHERS,
ITS TIME TO SET THE HATE ASIDE,
IF YWE WANT TO HAVE ETERNAL LIFE...

I CAN SEE THE PROPHECY,
I CAN SEE THE FUTURE AND WHAT IT ALL WILL BE,
LISTEN TO THIS PROPHECY
CAUSE IF THERE IS NO UNITY,
THEN THERE IS NO YOU AND ME

www.ingramcontent.com/pod-product-compliance
Lightning Source LLC
Chambersburg PA
CBHW080757120726

48001CB00009B/2781